OLEANNA

David Mamet

This play is dedicated to the memory of
Michael Merrit

**The Royal Court Writers Series published by
Methuen Drama in association with the Royal Court Theatre**

Royal Court Writers Series

Oleanna was first published in Great Britain
in the Royal Court Writers Series in 1993 by
Methuen Drama
in association with the Royal Court Theatre
Sloane Square, London SWIN 8AS
Methuen Publishing Limited
215 Vauxhall Bridge Road, London SWIV IEJ

This edition is offset from that first published in the United
States in hardcover by Pantheon Books and in paperback by Vintage
Books divisions of Random House, Inc, New York and simultaneously
in Canada by Random House of Canada Ltd, Toronto

20

Methuen Publishing Limited Reg. No. 3543167

ISBN 0-413-62620-2

A CIP catalogue record for this book
is available from the British Library

Printed and bound in Great Britain by
Cox & Wyman Ltd, Reading, Berkshire

Duke of York's Theatre
St Martin's Lane, London WC2N 4BG

Sole Proprietor and Licensee:
The Duke of York's Theatre Ltd

Directors: Sir Eddie Kulukundis OBE (Chairman),
Howard Panter (Managing Director), Peter Beckwith,
David Beresford Jones, Robin Guilleret.

Denis Lawson
Michelle Fairley

23310

oleanna

by David Mamet
directed by Harold Pinter

designed by Eileen Diss
lighting designed by Gerry Jenkinson

The Royal Court Theatre Production
presented by Graham Cowley for
Royal Court Theatre Productions Ltd
and the Oleanna New York Company

Originally produced on the stage by
THE BACK BAY THEATER COMPANY
in association with
AMERICAN REPERTORY THEATRE
Produced in New York by
FREDERICK ZOLLO   MITCHELL MAXWELL
ALAN J SCHUSTER   PEGGY HILL ROSENKRANZ
RON KASTNER   THOMAS VIERTEL STEVEN BARUCH
FRANK & WOJI GERO
in association with PATRICIA WOLFF
Associate Producers
D'ADDARIO SINE LTD   DAN MARKLEY   KEVIN McCOLLUM
Oleanna was originally produced as part of the Royal Court Theatre's American Season,
sponsored by AMERICAN AIRLINES and TIME OUT.

"Oh, to be in Oleanna - that's where I would rather be.
Than be bound in Norway and drag the chains of slavery."

American Folk Song

Rebecca Pidgeon and
William H Macy in
Oleanna at the
Orpheum Theatre,
New York 1992.

photo by Brigitte Lacombe

photo by John Haynes

Lia Williams and
David Suchet
in **Oleanna** at the
Royal Court Theatre,
London 1993.

First performed at the Hasty Pudding, Cambridge, Massachusetts
on 1 May 1992

First performance at the Orpheum Theatre, New York on
11 October 1992

First performance of this production at the Royal Court Theatre on
24 June 1993

First performance at the Duke of York's Theatre on
15 September 1993

First performance with this cast at the Duke of York's Theatre on
11 January 1994

The performance lasts approximately 2 hours 10 minutes

There will be one interval of fifteen minutes

There is a time lapse of one month between Acts One and Two

oleanna

by David Mamet

JOHN	**Denis Lawson**
CAROL	**Michelle Fairley**

Director	**Harold Pinter**
Designer	**Eileen Diss**
Lighting Designer	**Gerry Jenkinson**
Company Stage Manager	**Kim Ford**
Deputy Stage Manager	**Marian Spon**
Assistant Stage Manager	**Rose Blackshaw**
Assistant Director	**Mary Peate**
Casting	**Lisa Makin**
Production Manager	**Bo Barton**
Costume Supervisor	**Cathryn Johns**
Production Carpenter	**Guy Vlyyvrs**
Production Electrician	**Matthew O'Connor**
Voice Coach	**Charmian Hoare**
Fight Advisor	**Terry King**
Set built and painted by	**Ken Marples**
Production Photographer	**John Haynes**
Leaflet/Poster Design	**Loft**

The Royal Court would like to thank the following people: Briefcase supplied by **UDO**, pen supplied by **Parker Pens UK Ltd.**; books supplied by Oxford University Press and **The American College, London**; **Walton Street Stationery Company**; **Austin Tichenor**; **Tony Davies**; **Adelphi Graphics**; **Institute of Californian Wines**; wardrobe care by **Persil** and **Comfort**; hair by Carole at Edmond's, 19 Beauchamp Place, SW3; natural spring water from **Wye Spring Water**, 149 Sloane Street, London SW1, tel. 071-730 6977.

BIOGRAPHIES

DAVID MAMET

For the Royal Court: Oleanna, Edmond, The Shawl, Prairie du Chien.

Other plays include: Glengarry Glen Ross (Pulitzer Prize for Drama 1984, recently released as a film with Mamet screenplay); American Buffalo; A Life in the Theatre; Lakeboat; Reunion; Sexual Perversity in Chicago; The Water Engine; The Woods; Speed-The-Plow; Bobby Gould in Hell. Adaptation of Chekhov's Three Sisters (1991: Philadelphia Festival Theatre & Atlantic Theatre Company, New York).

Screenplays include: The Postman Always Rings Twice, The Verdict, The Untouchables, House of Games (which he also directed); Things Change (co-written with Shel Silverstein & directed); Homocide (directed); We're No Angels, Ace in the Hole, Deerslayer, High and Low, Hoffa.

Four books of essays include: Writing in Restaurants, On Directing Film, Some Freaks, The Cabin.

EILEEN DISS

For the Royal Court: Oleanna, Other theatre designs include: Blithe Spirit, The Philanderer, Watch on the Rhine, Measure for Measure, The Caretaker (Royal National Theatre); most of Simon Gray's plays (West End); The Seagull (Queens); Sweet Bird of Youth (Theatre Royal, Haymarket); Steel Magnolias (Lyric); The Mikado (Savoy); The Philanthropist (Wyndham's); The Caretaker (Comedy); The Hothouse, Rocket to the Moon, Translations, Circe & Bravo, Burn This (Hampstead); Private Lives, A Month in the Country (Gate, Dublin).

TV includes: Jeeves and Wooster; Best of Friends; Maigret; Somerset Maugham series; Cider With Rosie; Pygmalion; The Potting Shed; Hedda Gabler; The Prime of Miss Jean Brodie; Porterhouse Blue; Men Behaving Badly; Love on a Branch Line, many BBC Plays of the Month.

Feature films include: A Doll's House, Sweet William, Betrayal, 84 Charing Cross Road, A Handful of Dust.

MICHELLE FAIRLEY

Theatre includes: The Shadow of a Gunman (Irish & American tours); Leonce & Lena (Crucible, Sheffield); Factory Girls, Pentecost, The Hostage (Tricycle); The Doctor of Honour (Cheek by Jowl); By the Border (Royal National Theatre Studio); Don Juan (Royal Exchange, Manchester); Joyriders (Paines Plough); Philadelphia, Here I Come, Dr Faustus (Tron, Glasgow); Lady from the Sea (Citizens, Glasgow).

Television includes: Cross Fire, Hidden City, Saracens, Valentine Falls, Pentecost, Children of the North, Fleabites, Force of Duty, The Long Roads, Comics, Cardiac Arrest.

Film includes: Hidden Agenda.

GERRY JENKINSON

For the Royal Court: Oleanna, Colquhoun & MacBryde, Rocky Horror Show, Hamlet, The Normal Heart, Submariners, Glasshouses, Susan's Breasts, Jenkin's Ear.

Other theatre lighting designs include: For Services Rendered, Thee and Me, The Elephant Man, Translations, School for Wives, Yerma, The Duchess of Malfi, The White Devil, Martine, Entertaining Strangers, The Tempest, Cymbeline, A Winter's Tale (Royal National Theatre); Happy End, Taming of the

Shrew, Breaking the Silence,
The Revengers Tragedy, A
Woman of No Importance (RSC);
On the Verge, Ghosts, Romeo
and Juliet (National Theatre of
Norway); Rocky Horror Show;
Dusa, Fish, Stas and Vi; Bodies,
Clouds; Gloo Joo; The Hothouse;
Pal Joey; Can't Pay Won't Pay;
Summit Conference; Strange
Inter-lude; Phaedra; Mother
Courage; The Vortex; Design for
Living; Heat of the Day; Travels
With My Aunt; Torch Song
Trilogy; A Madhouse in Goa;
The Normal Heart; The Black
Prince; The Original Phantom of
the Opera; A Woman of No
Importance; The Invisible Man
(West End); The Shaughran
(Abbey, Dublin); A Life
(Olympia, Dublin). Since 1969
has lit almost all Glasgow
Citizens Theatre productions
with many international tours.
Opera lighting designs include:
Falstaff (Glyndebourne); La
Traviata, The Barber of Seville,
The Merry Widow (Scottish
Opera); Threepenny Opera,
Orpheus and Euridice, Aida,
Masquer-ade, La Gioconda
(Opera North); Tamburlaine,
Rigoletto (Welsh National
Opera); Carmen (Kent Opera);
Lazarus (Swedish Folk Opera);
Abduction from the Seraglio
(Buxton Festival Opera).

DENIS LAWSON

For the Royal Court: Mrs
Grabowski's Academy, The
Lucky Chance.

Other Theatre includes: Pal Joey
(Half Moon & Albery); Ashes
(Bush); Mr Cinders (King's Head
& Fortune - Olivier Award for
Best Actor in a Musical); Lend
me a Tenor (Globe Theatre); Bits
of Lenny Bruce (King's Head);
Volpone (Almeida); Lust
(Haymarket).

Television includes: Dead Head,
That Uncertain Feeling, The Kit
Curran Radio Show, Love After
Lunch, One Way Out, The
Justice Game (Parts I & II),
Natural Lies.

Films include: Providence, The
Man in the Iron Mask, Star
Wars, The Empire Strikes Back,
Return of the Jedi, Local Hero.

HAROLD PINTER

For the Royal Court: Oleanna
(1993), The New World Order
(1991).

Other theatre directing credits
include: The Collection (co-
directed with Peter Hall/
Aldwych, 1962); The Lover and
The Dwarfs (Arts, 1963); The
Birthday Party (Aldwych,
1964); Exiles (Mermaid, 1970);
Butley (Criterion, 1971); Next
of Kin (Royal National Theatre,
1974); Otherwise Engaged
(Queens, 1975; New York,
1977); The Innocents (New York,
1977); Blithe Spirit (RNT,
1977); The Rear Column (Globe,
1978); Close of Play (RNT,
1979); The Hothouse
(Hampstead, 1980); Quarter-
maine's Terms (Queens, 1981);
Incident at Tulse Hill
(Hampstead, 1982); The Trojan
War Will Not Take Place (RNT,
1983); The Common Pursuit
(Lyric, 1984); One for the Road
(Lyric Studio, 1984); Sweet Bird
of Youth (Haymarket, 1985);
Circe and Bravo (Hampstead &
Wyndham's, 1987); Mountain
Language (RNT, 1988); Vanilla
(Lyric, 1990); The Caretaker
(Comedy Theatre, 1991); Party
Time (Almeida, 1991).

TV includes: The Rear Column
(1980); The Hothouse (1982);
Mountain Language (1988);
Party Time (1992).

Film: Butley (1973).

NT
ROYAL
NATIONAL
THEATRE

**Lyttelton Theatre
In repertoire until
23 February**

Stephen Daldry's "STUPENDOUS REVIVAL"
Independent

of

MACHINAL

by Sophie Treadwell

FIONA SHAW - BEST ACTRESS
Evening Standard Drama Awards 1993

"THE PERFORMANCE OF 1993"
The Times

"STUNNING…One of the finest things the National has ever done"
Sunday Times

Fiona Shaw. Photo: Donald Cooper

REALISM by David Mamet

*Most American theatrical workers are in thrall to the idea of **realism**. A very real urge to be truthful, to be **true** constrains them to judge their efforts and actions against an inchoate, which is to say against an **unspecified** standard of reality.*

That the standard is unspecified is important as it has become the explanation and excuse for any action or effort the artist feels disinclined to make. It becomes a peremptory challenge.

*A necessary response to the artist who says "It's not **true**" must be "True to what?"*

*Stanislavsky, and more notably, Vakhtangov suggested that - that to which the artist must be **true** is the aesthetic integrity of the play.*

*This places a huge responsibility on the artist. He or she faced with this charge - to care for the **scenic truth** - can no longer take refuge in a blanket dismissal or **endorsement** of anything on the grounds of its not being realistic.*

*In general, each facet of every production must be weighed and understood solely on the basis of its interrelationship to the other elements; on its service or lack of service to the meaning, the **action** of the play.*

*A chair is not **per se** truthful or untruthful. That one may say, "Yes, but it is a chair, an actual chair, people sit on it and I found it in a cafeteria, therefore it belongs in this play about a cafeteria," is beside the point. Why was that **particular** chair chosen? Just as that particular chair said something about the cafeteria **in** the cafeteria (its concern for looks over comfort, for economy over durability, etc.) so that chair, on stage, will say something **about the play**; so the question is: "What do you, the theatrical director, wish to say **about the play**?"*

*What does the chair mean **in the play**? Does it symbolize power? Then have **that** chair. Abasement? Possession, and so on. Choose the correspondingly appropriate chair. One might say, "Give it up, **it's just a chair**..." But, again, someone is going to **choose** it; shouldn't that someone **recognize** that he is consciously or unconsciously making a choice, and make the choice consciously, and in favour of an idea more specific to the play than the idea of "reality".*

*A conscious devotion to the **Idea** of a play is a concern for what Stanislavsky called the Scenic Truth, which is to say, the truth **in this particular scene**. The important difference between realism and truth, Scenic Truth, is the difference between acceptability and necessity, which is the difference between entertainment and Art.*

So what if the play is set in a cafeteria? A cafeteria has no objective reality, as far as we artists are concerned. Our question is **why** is the play set in a cafeteria, what does it mean that the play is set in a cafeteria, and what **aspect** of this cafeteria is important **to the meaning of the play**. Having determined that, we may discard immediately all other aspects of the cafeteria and concentrate **only** on that which puts forward the meaning of the play. E.g.: if, in our particular play, the cafeteria means a place where the hero is always open to surveillance, the designer can build a set which reflects the idea: inability to hide. If the meaning of the cafeteria is a place where reflection and rest are possible, the designer's work can reflect **these** ideas. In neither case is the designer's first question: "What does a cafeteria look like?" His first question is: "What does it mean **in this instance**?" This is a concern for scenic truth.

In devotion to this Scenic Truth the artist gives him-or herself a choice. In discarding the armor of realism he or she accepts the responsibility of making every choice in light of specific **meaning** - of making every choice assertive rather than protective. For, in this age, to make a "realistic" choice, to assert that such and such a choice was made because it is, in fact, **as it is in life** is to say no more than that the choice was made in such a way as to avoid any potential criticism.

Everything which does not put forward the meaning of the play impedes the meaning of the play. To do too much or too little is to mitigate and weaken the meaning. The acting, the design, the direction should all consist only of that bare minimum necessary to put forward the action. Anything else is embellishment.

The problem of realism in design and its deleterious effects should be studied as a guide to the similar problem in acting. Actors for the last thirty years have been hiding in a ludicrously incorrect understanding of the Stanislavsky system and employing incorrectly understood jargon as an excuse for not acting.

Almost **never** are the teachings of Stanislavsky employed as an incitement; they are offered as an excuse - a substitute for action. The purpose of the system was, and is, to **free** the actor from extraneous considerations and permit him or her to turn all of his or her concentration to the objective, which is not "this performance" but the **meaning** of the play.

The notions of objective, activity, moment, beat, and so on are all devoted toward reducing the scene to a specific action which is true to the author's intention, and physically capable of being performed. The purpose of these concepts is to incite the actor to act. They all prod the actor to answer the one question which is capable of freeing him from self-consciousness and permitting him or her to become an artist: "What am I doing?"

The purpose of the Stanislavsky system of thought was to permit the actor to freely give the truth, the highest truth, of him - or herself, to the ideas, to the words of the playwright. The system teaches specificity as a tool of release rather than constraint. To make the transition from realism to truth, from self-consciousness to creativity, the artist must learn how to be specific to **something greater than him - or herself** on different levels of abstraction: the meaning of the scene, the intention of the author, the thrust of the play. But never the "reality" or "truth", in general.

That to which one must learn to be true is not one's vision of reality, which, by its very nature, will make the actor more self-conscious and less able to act, but the **aspirations** central to the meaning of the play and expressed in the objectives of the characters.

All theater is about aspirations - it is about longing and the desire for answers - small theater concerns itself with small questions, and great theater with great. In any case, the question at stake is never the **comfort** of the artist.

To have this never-ceasing concern with one's personal comfort, with the "naturalness" of the script, the blocking, the direction, the other actors, is to reduce every play to the **same** play - to a play about "That which I am not prepared to do" or "Those choices I will not make, and which I cannot be **forced** to make."

And so what?

Let us cast aside concerns of comfortability on stage. Why should one be comfortable acting Othello or St. Joan? The study of all theatrical artists should be action. **Movement**. A first test of all elements should be not "Do I feel comfortable (i.e., **immobile**) when considering it?" but "Do I feel **impelled**? Do I start to **move**? Does it make me want to **do** something?"

Actors are many times afraid of feeling foolish. We should teach each other to feel **power** rather than fear when faced with the necessity of choice, to seek out and enjoy, to feel the life-giving pleasure of the power of artistic choice.

This is one essay taken from a collection called "Life In The Theatre" from a book by David Mamet called "Writing In Restaurants". This was published in 1986 by Faber and Faber Ltd., who gave us their kind permission to reproduce it.

THE ENGLISH STAGE COMPANY AT THE ROYAL COURT THEATRE

The English Stage Company was formed to bring serious writing back to the stage. The Court's first Artistic Director, George Devine, wanted to create a vital and popular theatre. In order to promote this, he encouraged new writing that explored subjects drawn from contemporary life as well as pursuing European plays and forgotten classics. When John Osborne's **Look Back In Anger** was first produced in 1956, and revived in '57, it forced British Theatre into the modern age. At the same time Brecht, Giraudoux, Ionesco and Sartre were also part of the repertoire.

The ambition to discover new work which was challenging, innovative and also of the highest quality became the fulcrum of the Company's course of action. Early Court writers included Arnold Wesker, John Arden, David Storey, Ann Jellicoe, N F Simpson and Edward Bond. They were followed by a

generation of writers led by David Hare and Howard Brenton, and in more recent years, celebrated house writers have included Caryl Churchill, Timberlake Wertenbaker, Robert Holman and Jim Cartwright. Many of their plays are now regarded as modern classics.

In line with the policy of nurturing new writing, the Theatre Upstairs has mainly been seen as a place for exploration and experiment, where writers learn and develop their skills prior to the demands of the Main stage auditorium. Anne Devlin, Andrea Dunbar, Sarah Daniels, Jim Cartwright, Clare McIntyre, Winsome Pinnnock, and more recently Martin Crimp have, or will in the future, benefit from this process. The Theatre Upstairs proved its value as a focal point for new work with the production of the Chilean writer, Ariel Dorfman's **Death and the Maiden**

More recently, talented young writers as diverse as Jonathan Harvey, Adam Pernak, Phyllis Nagy (in association with the Liverpool Playhouse) and Gregory Motton (in association with the Royal National Theatre Studio) have been shown to great advantage in this space.

1991, 1992, and 1993 have been record-breaking years at the box-office with capacity houses for productions of **Top Girls**, **Three Birds Alighting on a Field**, **Faith Healer**, **Death and the Maiden** (which moved to The Duke of York's), **Six Degrees of Separation** (which moved to the Comedy Theatre) and most recently **King Lear** and, of course, **Oleanna**. **Death and the Maiden** and **Six Degrees of Separation** won the Olivier Award for Best Play in 1992 and 1993 respectively. **Three Birds Alighting on a Field** was awarded Best West End Play by the Writer's Guild of Great Britain, and has been successfully revived.

After nearly four decades, the Royal Court Theatre is still a major focus in the country for the production of new work. Scores of plays first seen in Sloane Square are now part of the National and International dramatic repertoire.

Photo: Mark Douet

Juliet Stevenson in **Death and the Maiden**

THE BACK BAY THEATER COMPANY

Started by David Mamet and Patricia Wolff. Oleanna was the company's inaugural production. Future projects include Hamlet, directed by Mamet, and his new adaptation of Anton Chekhov's The Seagull.

THE OLEANNA NEW YORK COMPANY

FREDERICK ZOLLO

Productions (with long time associate, Nicholas Paleologos) include: 'night Mother, On Golden Pond, Death and the Maiden, Talk Radio, Aven'U Boys, Marvin's Room, Angels in America (New York); Glengarry Glen Ross, Camille, Les Liasons Dangereuses, Death and the Maiden (London). Films include: Mississippi Burning, The Music of Chance, Quiz Show.

MITCHELL MAXWELL

President of Working Man Films Inc., and has presented on stage: Blues in the Night, Marvin's Room, Jeffrey, Key Exchange, Garden of Earthly Delights, Bouncers. Films include: The Lipstick Camera, Hand Gun, Matewan, Key Exchange. Next season Working Man Films will present a Broadway revival of the 1955 classic musical Damn Yankees, starring Bebe Neuwirth.

ALAN J SCHUSTER

Over 20 productions during the past 15 years on and Off-Broadway, on the road and in London. Last London production: Blues in the Night at the Piccadilly. Most recent New York productions include: Marvin's Room, Oleanna, Jeffrey. With his wife Pat and other intrepid urban pioneers rebuilt the Orpheum Theatre in 1978. With his partner Mitchell Maxwell built the Minetta Lane Theatre in 1984.

PEGGY HILL ROSENKRANZ

A lawyer who has practised entertainment, corporate and criminal law. Produced Raft of Medusa (1991) and is an assciate producer of the Tony Award-winning musical Jelly's Last Jam. Also a producer of Marvin's Room, winner of the 1992 Drama Desk Award for Best Play.

RON KASTNER

Producer or co-producer of sevral plays in New York and/or London including Tony Kushner's Angels in America, David Mamet's Oleanna, Ariel Dorfman's Death and the Maiden and Frank Pugliese's Aven'U Boys. Currently producing his first movie, White Man's Burden, directed by Gregory Hines.

THOMAS VIERTEL & STEVEN BARUCH

Began their producing partnership in 1985 with the original production of Penn & Teller. Produced, or co-produced, on and off-Broadway, in London and on national tour: Sills and Company (1986), Driving Miss Daisy and Frankie and Johnny in the Clair de Lune (1987), The Coctail Hour (1988) Love Letters (1989), Song of Singapore (1991), Marvin's Room and Oleanna (1992), and Jeffrey, Angels in America and Later Life (1993).

FRANK & WOJI GERO

Produced 16 plays in New York City including On Golden Pond, Key Exchange, Extremities and the six time Tony Award nominated Our Country's Good.. Since 1985 many plays in London including Breaking the Silence, Camille, Glengarry Glen Ross, the RSC Season at the Mermaid and the Royal Court's production of Our Country's Good (at the Garrick).

PATRICIA WOLFF

Currently the producer for David Mamet's film company Bay Kinescope and the Back Bay Theater Company. Member of the Atlantic Theater Co. Theatre credits include: Sketches of War, Live from the Empire Hotel. Films include: A Life in the Theatre (TNT).

D'ADDARIO/SINE LTD.

Jeffrey Sine is a Principal and head of the Media Group at Morgan Stanley & Co. Incorporated. Paul D'Addario is Senior Vice President at Donaldson, Fufkin & Jenrette Securities Corporation.

DAN MARKLEY

His company, ad hoc Productions produces many projects, including special events, concerts and television. Married to actress, Alison Sheehy.

KEVIN McCOLLUM

Owner and president of The Booking Office Inc., a New York based theatrical booking firm. Lives in New York City with his wife, actress Michele Pawk.

FOR THE ROYAL COURT THEATRE

Artistic Director	**Stephen Daldry**
General Manager	**Graham Cowley**
Finance Administrator	**Mark Rubinstein**
Casting Director	**Lisa Makin**
Literary Manager	**Robin Hooper**
Production Manager	**Bo Barton**
Master Carpenter	**Guy Viggers**
Chief Electrician	**Johanna Town**
Wardrobe Supervisor	**Jennifer Cook**
Marketing Manager	**Guy Chapman**
Press (071 730 2652)	**Anne Mayer**

The English Stage Company at the Royal Court Theatre receives funding from:
Arts Council of Great Britain, London Borough Grants Committee and The Royal Borough of Kensington and Chelsea.
It is the recipient of a grant from the Theatre Restoration Fund and from the Foundation for Sport & the Arts.
Its principal sponsors are: Barclays Bank, Marks & Spencer, British Gas North Thames, CitiBank, the Audrey Skirball-Kenis Theatre, The Rayne Foundation, Sir John Cass' Foundation, American Airlines.
Registered Charity Number 231242.

FOR ROYAL COURT THEATRE PRODUCTIONS

Directors
Stuart Burge CBE, **Anthony Burton, Graham Cowley, Harriet Cruickshank, Stephen Daldry, Robert Fox, Sonia Melchett, John Mortimer** QC **AG, Alan Rickman, Max Stafford-Clark.**

General Management	**Graham Cowley**
	Mark Rubinstein
Assisted by	**Rachel Harrison**
	Rebecca Shaw
Marketing (071 730 2652)	**Guy Chapman**
Sales/Marketing	**David Brownlee**
Press (Editorial - 071 383 5877)	
	Joy Sapieka Associates
Press (Review tickets - 071 730 2652)	**Anne Mayer**

THE AUDREY SKIRBALL-KENIS PLAYWRIGHTS PROGRAMME

Since it began in 1956, the aim of the English Stage Company has always been to develop and perform the best in new writing for the stage. In our present climate it is more important than ever for the Royal Court to adhere to these principles of development which have proved so successful in the past. **The Audrey Skirball-Kenis Playwrights Programme at the Royal Court** will allow us to expand this work.

The **Audrey Skirball-Kenis Theatre** is a non-profit arts service organisation based in Los Angeles. Since its founding in 1989 the ASK Theatre has sought to contribute to the quality, growth and vitality of theatre through the development of new writing for the stage. This mandate is being accomplished by offering comprehensive programmes and support services which provide direct assistance to playwrights. The Audrey Skirball-Kenis Playwrights Programme at the Royal Court is unique in its transatlantic connection. Through combinations of workshops, readings, dramaturgy, production without decor and commissioning, this new and creative programme will provide the opportunity for generations of writers to share their innovative ideas, aesthetics and working methods. In doing so these aims will not only benefit the programme of work presented at the Royal Court in the future, but also nourish contemporary theatre, nationally and internationally.

The Production of *Cleansed* owes its financial support received from The Theatre Investment Fund, a registered charity, which invests in many commercial productions, runs seminars for new producers and raises money for the commercial theatre. If you love the Theatre and wish to promote its future, please consider making a gift to the Fund. For further information regarding the Fund and its activities, please contact:
Chief Executive, Theatre Investment Fund Limited, The Palace Theatre, Shaftesbury Avenue, W1V 8AY. Telephone 071 287-2144.

FOR DUKE OF YORK'S THEATRE LTD

General Manager **Nicholas Wakeham**
Theatre Manager **James van Werven**
Management PA **Jenny Comber**
Accountant **Neil Davis**
Box Office Manager **Michele Harber**
(071 836 5122)
Master Carpenter **Max Alfonso**
Chief Electrician **Jerry Hodgson**
Stage Door **Kate Beard** (071 836 4615)

 For patrons who are hard of hearing, the Duke of York's Theatre has installed a Sennheiser Infra-Red Sound System.
Audio described performances take place at this theatre for patrons who are visually impaired. Described performances are provided by members of the London Audio Description Service (L.A.D.S.) - a voluntary organisation - in close association with the R.N.I.B.
Please contact the Box Office Manager for further details. Headphone units may be borrowed free of charge, on payment of a refundable deposit.

SMOKING IS STRICTLY FORBIDDEN IN THE AUDITORIUM

Please remember that noise such as whispering, coughing, the rustling of programmes and the bleeping of digital watches can be distracting to the performers and also spoils the performance for other members of the audience. All mobile phones and personal bleepers should be set to the OFF position.
Refreshments: for immediate service in the intervals, drinks may be ordered in advance at the bars. First aid facilities are provided by members of St John's Ambulance Brigade who give their services voluntarily. Patrons are reminded that the taking of photographs and use of any form of recording equipment is strictly forbidden during performances.
The Management reserve the right to refuse admission, also to make any alteration in the cast which may be rendered necessary by illness or other unavoidable causes.

In accordance with the requirements of the Licensing Authority: 1. The public may leave at the end of the performance or exhibition by all doors and such doors must at that time be kept open. 2. All gangways, corridors, staircases and external passageways intended for exit shall be kept entirely free from obstructions, whether permanent or temporary. 3. Persons shall not be permitted to stand in any of the gangways intersecting the seating or sit in any of the gangways. If standing be permitted in the gangways at the sides and rear of the seating, it shall be limited to the numbers indicated on the notices in those positiions. 4. The safety curtain must be lowered and raised in the presence of the audience.

ONE

□□□

JOHN *is talking on the phone.* CAROL *is seated across the desk from him.*

JOHN (*on phone*): And what about the land. (*Pause*) The land. And what about the land? (*Pause*) What about it? (*Pause*) No. I don't understand. Well, yes, I'm I'm . . . no, I'm *sure* it's signif . . . I'm sure it's significant. (*Pause*) Because it's significant to mmmmmm . . . did you call Jerry? (*Pause*) Because . . . no, no, no, no, no. What did they say . . . ? Did you speak to the *real* estate . . . where *is* she . . . ? Well, well, all right. Where are her notes? Where are the notes we took with her. (*Pause*) I thought you were? No. No, I'm sorry, I didn't mean that, I just thought that I saw you, when we were there . . . what . . . ? I thought I saw you with a *pencil*. WHY NOW? is what I'm say . . . well, that's why I say "call Jerry." Well, I can't right now, be . . . no, I *didn't*

1

schedule any . . . Grace: I *didn't* . . . I'm well aware . . . Look: Look. Did you call Jerry? Will you call Jerry . . . ? Because I can't now. I'll be there, I'm sure I'll be there in fifteen, in twenty. I intend to. No, we aren't *going* to lose the, we aren't *going* to lose the house. Look: Look, I'm not minimizing it. The "easement." Did she say "easement"? (*Pause*) What did she *say; is* it a "term of art," are we *bound* by it . . . I'm sorry . . . (*Pause*) are: we: yes. *Bound* by . . . Look: (*He checks his watch.*) before the other side *goes home,* all right? "a term of art." Because: that's right (*Pause*) The yard for the boy. Well, that's the whole . . . Look: I'm going to meet you there . . . (*He checks his watch.*) Is the realtor there? All right, tell her to show you the basement again. Look at the *this* because . . . Bec . . . I'm leaving in, I'm leaving in ten or fifteen . . . Yes. No, no, I'll meet you at the new . . . That's a good. If he thinks it's necc . . . you tell Jerry to meet . . . All right? We *aren't* going to lose the deposit. All right? I'm sure it's going to be . . . (*Pause*) I hope so. (*Pause*) I love you, too. (*Pause*) I love you, too. As soon as . . . I will.

(*He hangs up.*) (*He bends over the desk and makes a note.*) (*He looks up.*) (*To* CAROL:) I'm sorry . . .

CAROL: (*Pause*) What is a "term of art"?

JOHN: (*Pause*) I'm sorry . . . ?

CAROL: (*Pause*) What is a "term of art"?

JOHN: Is that what you want to talk about?

CAROL: . . . to talk about . . . ?

JOHN: Let's take the mysticism out of it, shall we? Carol? (*Pause*) Don't you think? I'll tell you: when you have some "thing." Which must be broached. (*Pause*) Don't you think . . . ? (*Pause*)

CAROL: . . . don't I think . . . ?

JOHN: Mmm?

CAROL: . . . did I . . . ?

JOHN: . . . what?

CAROL: Did . . . did I . . . did I say something wr . . .

JOHN: (*Pause*) No. I'm sorry. No. You're right. I'm very sorry. I'm somewhat rushed. As you see. I'm sorry. You're right. (*Pause*) What is a "term of art"? It seems to mean a *term*, which has come, through its use, to mean something *more specific* than the words would, to someone *not acquainted* with them . . . indicate. That, I believe, is what a "term of art," would mean. (*Pause*)

CAROL: You don't know what it means . . . ?

JOHN: I'm not sure that I know what it means. It's one of those things, perhaps you've had them, that, you look them up, or have someone explain them to you, and you say "aha," and, you immediately *forget* what . . .

CAROL: You don't do that.

JOHN: . . . I . . . ?

CAROL: You don't do . . .

JOHN: . . . I don't, what . . . ?

CAROL: . . . for . . .

JOHN: . . . I don't for . . .

CAROL: . . . no . . .

JOHN: . . . forget things? Everybody does that.

CAROL: No, they don't.

JOHN: They don't . . .

CAROL: No.

JOHN: (*Pause*) No. Everybody does that.

CAROL: Why would they do that . . . ?

JOHN: Because. I don't know. Because it doesn't interest them.

CAROL: No.

JOHN: I think so, though. (*Pause*) I'm sorry that I was distracted.

CAROL: You don't have to say that to me.

JOHN: You paid me the compliment, or the "obeisance"—all right—of coming in here . . . All right. *Carol*. I find that I am at a *standstill*. I find that I . . .

CAROL: . . . what . . .

JOHN: . . . one moment. In regard to your . . . to your . . .

CAROL: Oh, oh. You're buying a new house!

JOHN: No, let's get on with it.

CAROL: "get on"? (*Pause*)

JOHN: I know how . . . *believe* me. I know how . . . potentially *humiliating* these . . . I have no desire to . . . I have no desire other than to help you. But: (*He picks up some papers on his desk.*) I won't even say "but." I'll say that as I go back over the . . .

CAROL: I'm just, I'm just trying to . . .

JOHN: . . . no, it will not do.

CAROL: . . . what? What will . . . ?

JOHN: No. I see, I see what you, it . . . (*He gestures to the papers.*) but your work . . .

CAROL: I'm just: I sit in class I . . . (*She holds up her notebook.*) I take notes . . .

JOHN (*simultaneously with* "notes"): Yes. I understand. What I am trying to *tell* you is that some, some basic . . .

CAROL: . . . I . . .

JOHN: . . . one moment: some basic missed communi . . .

CAROL: I'm doing what I'm told. I bought your book, I read your . . .

JOHN: No, I'm sure you . . .

CAROL: No, no, no. I'm doing what I'm told. It's *difficult* for me. It's *difficult* . . .

JOHN: . . . but . . .

CAROL: I don't . . . lots of the *language* . . .

JOHN: . . . please . . .

CAROL: The *language,* the "things" that you say . . .

JOHN: I'm sorry. No. I don't think that that's true.

CAROL: It *is* true. I . . .

JOHN: I think . . .

CAROL: It *is* true.

JOHN: . . . I . . .

CAROL: Why would I . . . ?

JOHN: I'll tell you why: you're an incredibly bright girl.

CAROL: . . . I . . .

JOHN: You're an incredibly . . . you have no problem with the . . . Who's kidding who?

CAROL: . . . I . . .

JOHN: No. No. I'll tell you why. I'll tell . . . . I think you're *angry*, I . . .

CAROL: . . . why would I . . .

JOHN: . . . wait one moment. I . . .

CAROL: It *is* true. I have *problems* . . .

JOHN: . . . every . . .

CAROL: . . . I come from a different *social* . . .

JOHN: . . . ev . . .

CAROL: a different economic . . .

JOHN: . . . Look:

CAROL: No. I: when I *came* to this school:

JOHN: Yes. Quite . . . (*Pause*)

CAROL: . . . does that mean nothing . . . ?

JOHN: . . . but look: look . . .

CAROL: . . . I . . .

JOHN: (*Picks up paper.*) Here: Please: Sit down. (*Pause*)
Sit down. (*Reads from her paper.*) "I think that the
ideas contained in this work express the author's
feelings in a way that he intended, based on his
results." What can that mean? Do you see?
What . . .

CAROL: I, the best that I . . .

JOHN: I'm saying, that perhaps this course . . .

CAROL: No, no, no, you can't, you can't . . . I have
to . . .

JOHN: . . . how . . .

CAROL: . . . I have to pass it . . .

JOHN: Carol, I:

CAROL: I *have* to pass this course, I . . .

JOHN: Well.

CAROL: . . . don't you . . .

JOHN: Either the . . .

CAROL: . . . I . . .

JOHN: . . . either the, I . . . either the *criteria* for judging progress in the class are . . .

CAROL: No, no, no, no, I have to pass it.

JOHN: Now, look: I'm a human being, I . . .

CAROL: I did what you told me. I did, I did everything that, I read your *book,* you told me to buy your book and read it. Everything you *say* I . . . (*She gestures to her notebook.*) (*The phone rings.*) I do. . . . Ev . . .

JOHN: . . . look:

CAROL: . . . everything I'm told . . .

JOHN: Look. Look. I'm not your *father.* (*Pause*)

CAROL: What?

JOHN: I'm.

CAROL: Did I say you were my father?

JOHN: . . . no . . .

CAROL: Why did you say that . . . ?

JOHN: I . . .

CAROL: . . . why . . . ?

JOHN: . . . in class I . . . (*He picks up the phone.*) (*Into phone:*) Hello. I can't talk now. Jerry? Yes? I underst . . . I can't talk now. I know . . . I know . . . Jerry. I can't *talk* now. Yes, I. Call me back in . . . Thank you. (*He hangs up.*) (*To* CAROL:) What do you want me to do? We are two people, all right? Both of whom have subscribed to . . .

CAROL: No, no . . .

JOHN: . . . certain arbitrary . . .

CAROL: No. You have to help me.

JOHN: Certain institutional . . . you tell me what you want me to do. . . . You tell me what you want me to . . .

CAROL: How can I go back and tell them the *grades* that I . . .

JOHN: . . . what can I do . . . ?

CAROL: *Teach* me. *Teach* me.

JOHN: . . . I'm trying to teach you.

CAROL: I read your book. I read it. I don't under . . .

JOHN: . . . you don't understand it.

CAROL: No.

JOHN: Well, perhaps it's not well *written* . . .

CAROL (*simultaneously with* "written"): No. No. No. I want to *understand* it.

JOHN: What don't you understand? (*Pause*)

CAROL: *Any* of it. What you're trying to say. When you talk about . . .

JOHN: . . . yes . . . ? (*She consults her notes.*)

CAROL: "Virtual warehousing of the young" . . .

JOHN: "Virtual warehousing of the young." If we artificially prolong adolescence . . .

CAROL: . . . and about "The Curse of Modern Education."

JOHN: . . . well . . .

CAROL: I don't . . .

JOHN: Look. It's just a *course*, it's just a *book*, it's just a . . .

CAROL: No. No. There are *people* out there. People who came *here*. To know something they didn't *know*. Who *came* here. To be *helped*. To be *helped*. So someone would *help* them. To *do* something. To *know* something. To get, what do they say? "To get on in the world." How can I do that if I don't, if I fail? But I don't *understand*. I don't *understand*. I don't understand what anything means . . . and I walk around. From morning 'til night: with this one thought in my head. I'm *stupid*.

JOHN: No one thinks you're stupid.

CAROL: No? What am I . . . ?

JOHN: I . . .

CAROL: . . . what am I, then?

JOHN: I think you're angry. Many people are. I have a *telephone* call that I have to make. And an *ap-*

pointment, which is rather *pressing;* though I sympathize with your concerns, and though I wish I had the time, this was not a previously scheduled meeting and I . . .

CAROL: . . . you think I'm nothing . . .

JOHN: . . . have an appointment with a *realtor,* and with my wife and . . .

CAROL: You think that I'm stupid.

JOHN: No. I certainly don't.

CAROL: You said it.

JOHN: No. I did not.

CAROL: You did.

JOHN: When?

CAROL: . . . you . . .

JOHN: No. I never did, or never would say that to a student, and . . .

CAROL: You said, "What can that mean?" (*Pause*) "What can that mean?" . . . (*Pause*)

JOHN: . . . and what did that mean to you . . . ?

CAROL: That meant I'm stupid. And I'll never learn. That's what that meant. And you're right.

JOHN: . . . I . . .

CAROL: But then. But then, what am I doing here . . . ?

JOHN: . . . if you thought that I . . .

CAROL: . . . when nobody wants me, and . . .

JOHN: . . . if you interpreted . . .

CAROL: Nobody *tells* me anything. And I *sit* there . . . in the *corner*. In the *back*. And everybody's talking about "this" all the time. And "concepts," and "precepts" and, and, and, and, and, WHAT IN THE WORLD ARE YOU *TALKING* ABOUT? And I read your book. And they said, "Fine, go in that class." Because you talked about responsibility to the young. I DON'T KNOW WHAT IT MEANS AND I'M *FAILING* . . .

JOHN: May . . .

CAROL: No, you're right. "Oh, hell." I failed. Flunk me out of it. It's garbage. Everything I do. "The ideas contained in this work express the author's feelings." That's right. That's right. I know I'm stupid. I know what I am. (*Pause*) I know what

I am, Professor. You don't have to tell me. (*Pause*) It's pathetic. Isn't it?

JOHN: . . . Aha . . . (*Pause*) Sit down. Sit down. Please. (*Pause*) Please sit down.

CAROL: Why?

JOHN: I want to talk to you.

CAROL: Why?

JOHN: Just sit down. (*Pause*) Please. Sit down. Will you, please . . . ? (*Pause. She does so.*) Thank you.

CAROL: What?

JOHN: I want to tell you something.

CAROL: (*Pause*) What?

JOHN: Well, I know what you're talking about.

CAROL: No. You don't.

JOHN: I think I do. (*Pause*)

CAROL: How can you?

JOHN: I'll tell you a story about myself. (*Pause*) Do you mind? (*Pause*) I was raised to think myself stupid. That's what I want to tell you. (*Pause*)

CAROL: What do you mean?

JOHN: Just what I said. I was brought up, and my earliest, and most persistent memories are of being told that I was stupid. "You have such *intelligence*. Why must you behave so *stupidly*?" Or, "Can't you *understand?* Can't you *understand*?" And I could *not* understand. I could *not* understand.

CAROL: What?

JOHN: The simplest problem. Was beyond me. It was a mystery.

CAROL: What was a mystery?

JOHN: How people learn. How *I* could learn. Which is what I've been speaking of in class. And of *course* you can't hear it. Carol. Of *course* you can't. (*Pause*) I used to speak of "real people," and wonder what the *real* people did. The *real* people. Who were they? *They* were the people other than myself. The *good* people. The *capable* people. The people who could do the things, *I* could not do: learn, study, retain . . . all that *garbage*—which is what I have been talking of in class, and that's *exactly* what I have been talking of—If you are told . . . . Listen to this. If the young child is told he cannot understand. Then he takes it as a *description* of himself. What am I? I am *that which can not understand*. And I saw you out there, when we were speaking of the con-cepts of . . .

CAROL: I can't understand any of them.

JOHN: Well, then, that's *my* fault. That's not your fault. And that is not verbiage. That's what I firmly hold to be the truth. And I am sorry, and I owe you an apology.

CAROL: Why?

JOHN: And I suppose that I have had some *things* on my mind. . . . We're buying a *house,* and . . .

CAROL: People said that you were stupid . . . ?

JOHN: Yes.

CAROL: When?

JOHN: I'll tell you when. Through my life. In my childhood; and, perhaps, they stopped. But I heard them continue.

CAROL: And what did they say?

JOHN: They said I was incompetent. Do you see? And when I'm tested the, the, the *feelings* of my youth about the *very subject of learning* come up. And I . . . I become, I feel "unworthy," and "unpre-pared." . . .

CAROL: . . . yes.

JOHN: . . . eh?

CAROL: . . . yes.

JOHN: And I feel that I must fail. (*Pause*)

CAROL: . . . but then you *do* fail. (*Pause*) You have to. (*Pause*) Don't you?

JOHN: A *pilot*. Flying a plane. The pilot is flying the plane. He thinks: Oh, my *God*, my mind's been drifting! Oh, my God! What kind of a cursed imbecile am I, that I, with this so precious cargo of *Life* in my charge, would allow my attention to wander. Why was I born? How deluded are those who put their trust in me, . . . et cetera, so on, and he crashes the plane.

CAROL: (*Pause*) He could just . . .

JOHN: That's right.

CAROL: He could say:

JOHN: My attention *wandered* for a moment . . .

CAROL: . . . uh huh . . .

JOHN: I had a *thought* I did not like . . . but now:

CAROL: . . . but now it's . . .

JOHN: That's what I'm telling you. It's time to put my attention . . . see: it is not: this is what I learned. It is Not Magic. Yes. Yes. *You*. You are going to be frightened. When faced with what may or may not be but which you are going to perceive as a test. You will become frightened. And you will say: "I am incapable of . . ." and everything *in* you will think these two things. "I must. But I can't." And you will think: Why was I born to be the laughingstock of a world in which everyone is better than I? In which I am entitled to nothing. Where I can not learn.

(*Pause*)

CAROL: Is that . . . (*Pause*) Is that what I have . . . ?

JOHN: Well. I don't know if I'd put it that way. Listen: I'm talking to you as I'd talk to my son. Because that's what I'd like him to have that I never had. I'm talking to you the way I wish that someone had talked to me. I don't know how to do it, other than to be *personal*, . . . but . . .

CAROL: Why would you want to be personal with me?

JOHN: Well, you see? That's what I'm saying. We can only interpret the behavior of others through the screen we . . . (*The phone rings*.) Through . . . (*To phone:*) Hello . . . ? (*To* CAROL:) Through the screen we create. (*To phone:*) Hello. (*To* CAROL:) Excuse me a moment. (*To phone:*) Hello? No, I can't talk nnn . . . I know I did. In a few . . . I'm . . . is he coming to the . . . yes. I talked to him. We'll meet you at the No, because I'm with a *student*. It's going to be fff . . . This is important, too. I'm with a *student,* Jerry's going to . . . Listen: the sooner I get off, the sooner I'll be down, all right. I love you. Listen, listen, I said "I love you," it's going to work *out* with the, because I feel that it is, I'll be right down. All right? Well, then it's going to take as long as it takes. (*He hangs up.*) (*To* CAROL:) I'm sorry.

CAROL: What was that?

JOHN: There are some problems, as there usually are, about the final agreements for the new house.

CAROL: You're buying a new house.

JOHN: That's right.

CAROL: Because of your promotion.

JOHN: Well, I suppose that that's right.

CAROL: Why did you stay here with me?

JOHN: Stay here.

CAROL: Yes. When you should have gone.

JOHN: Because I like you.

CAROL: You like me.

JOHN: Yes.

CAROL: Why?

JOHN: Why? Well? Perhaps we're similar. (*Pause*) Yes. (*Pause*)

CAROL: You said "everyone has problems."

JOHN: Everyone has problems.

CAROL: Do they?

JOHN: Certainly.

CAROL: You do?

JOHN: Yes.

CAROL: What are they?

JOHN: Well. (*Pause*) Well, you're perfectly right (*Pause*) If we're going to take off the Artificial *Stricture*, of "Teacher," and "Student," why should *my* problems be any more a mystery than your own? Of *course* I have problems. As you saw.

CAROL: . . . with what?

JOHN: With my *wife* . . . with *work* . . .

CAROL: With work?

JOHN: Yes. And, and, perhaps my problems are, do you see? *Similar* to yours.

CAROL: Would you tell me?

JOHN: All right. (*Pause*) I came *late* to teaching. And I found it Artificial. The notion of "I know and you do not"; and I saw an *exploitation* in the education process. I told you. I hated school, I hated teachers. I hated everyone who was in the position of a "boss" because I *knew*—I didn't *think,* mind you, I *knew* I was going to fail. Because I was a fuckup. I was just no goddamned good. When I . . . late in life . . . (*Pause*) When I *got out from under* . . . when I worked my way out of the need to fail. When I . . .

CAROL: How do you do that? (*Pause*)

JOHN: You have to look at what you are, and what you feel, and how you act. And, finally, you have to look at how you act. And say: If that's what I *did,* that must be how I think of myself.

CAROL: I don't understand.

JOHN: If I fail all the time, it must be that I think of myself as a failure. If I do not want to think of myself as a failure, perhaps I should begin by *succeeding* now and again. Look. The tests, you see, which you encounter, in school, in college, in life, were designed, in the most part, for idiots. *By* idiots. There is no need to fail at them. They are not a test of your worth. They are a test of your ability to retain and spout back misinformation. Of *course* you fail them. They're *nonsense*. And I . . .

CAROL: . . . no . . .

JOHN: Yes. They're *garbage*. They're a *joke*. Look at me. Look at me. The Tenure Committee. The Tenure Committee. Come to judge me. The Bad Tenure Committee.

The "Test." Do you see? They put me to the test. Why, they had people voting on me I wouldn't employ to wax my car. And yet, I go before the Great Tenure Committee, and I have an urge, to *vomit,* to, to, to puke my *badness* on the table, to show them: "I'm no good. Why would you pick *me?*"

CAROL: They granted you tenure.

JOHN: Oh no, they announced it, but they haven't *signed*. Do you see? "At any moment . . ."

CAROL: . . . mmm . . .

JOHN: "They might not *sign*" . . . I might not . . . the *house* might not go through . . . Eh? Eh? They'll find out my "dark secret." (*Pause*)

CAROL: . . . what is it . . . ?

JOHN: There *isn't* one. But *they* will find an index of my badness . . .

CAROL: Index?

JOHN: A ". . . pointer." A "Pointer." You see? Do you see? I *understand* you. I. Know. That. Feeling. Am I entitled to my job, and my nice *home,* and my *wife,* and my *family,* and so on. This is what I'm saying: That theory of education which, that *theory:*

CAROL: I . . . I . . . (*Pause*)

JOHN: What?

CAROL: I . . .

JOHN: What?

CAROL: I want to know about my grade. (*Long pause*)

JOHN: Of course you do.

CAROL: Is that bad?

JOHN: No.

CAROL: Is it bad that I asked you that?

JOHN: No.

CAROL: Did I upset you?

JOHN: No. And I apologize. Of *course* you want to know about your grade. And, of course, you can't concentrate on anyth . . . (*The telephone starts to ring.*) Wait a moment.

CAROL: I should go.

JOHN: I'll make you a deal.

CAROL: No, you have to . . .

JOHN: Let it ring. I'll make you a deal. You stay here. We'll start the whole course over. I'm going to say it was not you, it was I who was not paying attention. We'll start the whole course over. Your grade is an "A." Your final grade is an "A." (*The phone stops ringing.*)

CAROL: But the class is only half over . . .

JOHN (*simultaneously with* "over"): Your grade for the whole term is an "A." If you will come back and meet with me. A few more times. Your grade's an "A." Forget about the paper. You didn't like it, you didn't like writing it. It's not important.

What's important is that I awake your interest, if I can, and that I answer your questions. Let's start over. (*Pause*)

CAROL: Over. With what?

JOHN: Say this is the beginning.

CAROL: The beginning.

JOHN: Yes.

CAROL: Of what?

JOHN: Of the class.

CAROL: But we can't start over.

JOHN: I say we can. (*Pause*) I say we can.

CAROL: But I don't believe it.

JOHN: Yes, I know that. But it's true. What is The Class but you and me? (*Pause*)

CAROL: There are rules.

JOHN: Well. We'll break them.

CAROL: How can we?

JOHN: We won't tell anybody.

CAROL: Is that all right?

JOHN: I say that it's fine.

CAROL: Why would you do this for me?

JOHN: I like you. Is that so difficult for you to . . .

CAROL: Um . . .

JOHN: There's no one here but you and me. (*Pause*)

CAROL: All right. I did not understand. When you
referred . . .

JOHN: All right, yes?

CAROL: When you referred to hazing.

JOHN: Hazing.

CAROL: You wrote, in your book. About the comparative . . . the comparative . . . (*She checks her
notes.*)

JOHN: Are you checking your notes . . . ?

CAROL: Yes.

JOHN: Tell me in your own . . .

CAROL: I want to make sure that I have it right.

JOHN: No. Of course. You want to be exact.

CAROL: I want to know everything that went on.

JOHN: . . . that's good.

CAROL: . . . so I . . .

JOHN: That's very good. But I was suggesting, many times, that that which we wish to retain is retained oftentimes, I think, *better* with less expenditure of effort.

CAROL: (*Of notes*) Here it is: you wrote of *hazing*.

JOHN: . . . that's correct. Now: I said "hazing." It means ritualized annoyance. We shove this book at you, we say read it. Now, you say you've read it? I think that you're *lying*. I'll *grill* you, and when I find you've lied, you'll be disgraced, and your life will be ruined. It's a sick game. Why do we do it? Does it educate? In no sense. Well, then, what is higher education? It is something-other-than-useful.

CAROL: What is "something-other-than-useful?"

JOHN: It has become a ritual, it has become an article of faith. That all must be subjected to, or to put it differently, that all are entitled to Higher Education. And my point . . .

CAROL: You disagree with that?

JOHN: Well, let's address that. What do you think?

CAROL: I don't know.

JOHN: What do you think, though? (*Pause*)

CAROL: I don't know.

JOHN: I spoke of it in class. Do you remember my example?

CAROL: Justice.

JOHN: Yes. Can you repeat it to me? (*She looks down at her notebook.*) Without your notes? I ask you as a favor to me, so that I can see if my idea was interesting.

CAROL: You said "justice" . . .

JOHN: Yes?

CAROL: . . . that all are entitled . . . (*Pause*) I . . . I . . . I . . .

JOHN: Yes. To a speedy trial. To a fair trial. But they needn't be given a trial *at all* unless they stand accused. Eh? Justice is their right, should they choose to avail themselves of it, they should have a fair trial. It does not follow, of necessity, a person's life is incomplete without a trial in it. Do you see?

My point is a confusion between equity and *utility* arose. So we confound the *usefulness* of higher education with our, granted, right to equal access to the same. We, in effect, create a *prejudice* toward it, completely independent of . . .

CAROL: . . . that it is prejudice that we should go to school?

JOHN: Exactly. (*Pause*)

CAROL: How can you say that? How . . .

JOHN: Good. Good. *Good*. That's right! Speak up! What is a prejudice? An unreasoned belief. We are all subject to it. None of us is not. When it is threatened, or opposed, we feel anger, and feel, do we not? As you do now. Do you not? Good.

CAROL: . . . but how can you . . .

JOHN: . . . let us examine. Good.

CAROL: How . . .

JOHN: Good. Good. When . . .

CAROL: I'M SPEAKING . . . (*Pause*)

JOHN: I'm sorry.

CAROL: How can you . . .

JOHN: . . . I beg your pardon.

CAROL: That's all right.

JOHN: I beg your pardon.

CAROL: That's all right.

JOHN: I'm sorry I interrupted you.

CAROL: That's all right.

JOHN: You were saying?

CAROL: I was saying . . . I was saying . . . (*She checks her notes*.) How can you say in a class. Say in a college class, that college education is prejudice?

JOHN: I said that our predilection for it . . .

CAROL: Predilection . . .

JOHN: . . . you know what that means

CAROL: Does it mean "liking"?

JOHN: Yes.

CAROL: But how can you say that? That College . . .

JOHN: . . . that's my *job,* don't you know.

CAROL: What is?

JOHN: To provoke you.

CAROL: No.

JOHN: Oh. Yes, though.

CAROL: To provoke me?

JOHN: That's right.

CAROL: To make me mad?

JOHN: That's right. To force you . . .

CAROL: . . . to make me mad is your job?

JOHN: To force you to . . . listen: (*Pause*) Ah. (*Pause*) When I was young somebody told me, are you ready, the rich copulate less often than the poor. But when they do, they take more of their clothes off. Years. Years, mind you, I would compare experiences of my own to this dictum, saying, aha, this fits the norm, or ah, this is a variation from it. What did it mean? Nothing. It was some jerk thing, some school kid told me that took up room inside my head. (*Pause*)

Somebody told *you,* and you hold it as an article of faith, that higher education is an unassailable good. This notion is so dear to you that when I question it you become angry. Good. Good, I say. Are not those the very things which we should question? I say college education, since the war, has become so a matter of course, and such a fashionable necessity, for those either of or aspiring *to* to the new vast middle class, that we *espouse* it, as a matter of right, and have ceased to ask, "What is it good for?" (*Pause*)

What might be some reasons for pursuit of higher education?
One: A love of learning.
Two: The wish for mastery of a skill.
Three: For economic betterment.
(*Stops. Makes a note.*)

CAROL: I'm keeping you.

JOHN: One moment. I have to make a note . . .

CAROL: It's something that I said?

JOHN: No, we're buying a house.

CAROL: You're buying the new house.

JOHN: To go with the tenure. That's right. Nice *house,* close to the *private school* . . . (*He continues making his note.*) . . . We were talking of economic *betterment* (CAROL *writes in her notebook.*) . . . I was thinking of the School Tax. (*He contin-*

ues writing.) (*To himself:*) . . . *where is it written* that
I have to send my child to public school. . . . Is
it a law that I have to improve the City Schools
at the expense of my own interest? And, is this
not simply *The White Man's Burden?* Good. And
(*Looks up to* CAROL) . . . does this interest you?

CAROL: No. I'm taking notes . . .

JOHN: You don't have to take notes, you know, you
can just listen.

CAROL: I want to make sure I remember it. (*Pause*)

JOHN: I'm not lecturing you, I'm just trying to tell
you some things I think.

CAROL: What do you think?

JOHN: Should all kids go to college? *Why* . . .

CAROL: (*Pause*) To learn.

JOHN: But if he does not learn.

CAROL: If the child does not learn?

JOHN: Then why is he in college? Because he was told
it was his "right"?

CAROL: Some might find college instructive.

JOHN: I would hope so.

CAROL: But how do they feel? Being told they are wasting their time?

JOHN: I don't think I'm telling them that.

CAROL: You said that education was "prolonged and systematic hazing."

JOHN: Yes. It can be so.

CAROL: . . . if education is so *bad*, why do you do it?

JOHN: I do it because I love it. (*Pause*) Let's . . . . I suggest you look at the demographics, wage-earning capacity, college- and non-college-educated men and women, 1855 to 1980, and let's see if we can wring some worth from the statistics. Eh? And . . .

CAROL: No.

JOHN: What?

CAROL: I can't understand them.

JOHN: . . . you . . . ?

CAROL: . . . the "charts." The *Concepts*, the . . .

JOHN: "Charts" are simply . . .

CAROL: When I leave here . . .

JOHN: Charts, do you see . . .

CAROL: No, I can't . . .

JOHN: You can, though.

CAROL: NO, NO—I DON'T UNDERSTAND. DO YOU SEE??? I DON'T *UNDER-STAND* . . .

JOHN: What?

CAROL: *Any* of it. *Any* of it. I'm *smiling* in class, I'm *smiling,* the whole time. What are you *talking* about? What is everyone *talking* about? I don't *understand.* I don't know what it *means.* I don't know what it means to *be* here . . . you tell me I'm intelligent, and then you tell me I should not be *here,* what do you *want* with me? What does it *mean?* Who should I *listen* to . . . I . . .

(*He goes over to her and puts his arm around her shoulder.*)

NO! (*She walks away from him.*)

JOHN: Sshhhh.

CAROL: No, I don't under . . .

JOHN: Sshhhhh.

CAROL: I don't know what you're *saying* . . .

JOHN: Sshhhhh. It's all right.

CAROL: . . . I have no . . .

JOHN: Sshhhhh. Sshhhhh. Let it go a moment. (*Pause*) Sshhhhh . . . let it go. (*Pause*) Just let it go. (*Pause*) Just let it go. It's all right. (*Pause*) Sshhhhh. (*Pause*) I understand . . . (*Pause*) What do you feel?

CAROL: I feel bad.

JOHN: I know. It's all right.

CAROL: I . . . (*Pause*)

JOHN: What?

CAROL: I . . .

JOHN: What? Tell me.

CAROL: I don't understand you.

JOHN: I know. It's all right.

CAROL: I . . .

JOHN: What? (*Pause*) What? *Tell* me.

CAROL: I can't tell you.

JOHN: No, you must.

CAROL: I can't.

JOHN: No. Tell me. (*Pause*)

CAROL: I'm bad. (*Pause*) Oh, God. (*Pause*)

JOHN: It's all right.

CAROL: I'm . . .

JOHN: It's all right.

CAROL: I can't talk about this.

JOHN: It's all right. Tell me.

CAROL: Why do you want to know this?

JOHN: I don't want to know. I want to know whatever you . . .

CAROL: I always . . .

JOHN: . . . good . . .

CAROL: I always . . . all my life . . . I have never told anyone this . . .

JOHN: Yes. Go on. (*Pause*) Go on.

CAROL: All of my life . . . (*The phone rings.*) (*Pause.* JOHN *goes to the phone and picks it up.*)

JOHN (*into phone*): I can't talk now. (*Pause*) What? (*Pause*) Hmm. (*Pause*) All right, I . . . I. Can't.

Talk. Now. No, no, no, I *Know* I did, but
. . . . What? Hello. What? She *what?* She *can't,*
she said the agreement is void? How, how is the
agreement *void? That's Our House.*

I have the *paper;* when we come down, next
week, with the payment, and the paper, that
house is . . . wait, wait, wait, wait, wait, wait,
wait: Did Jerry . . . is Jerry there? (*Pause*) Is *she*
there . . . ? Does she have a *lawyer* . . . ? How the
hell, how the *Hell.* That is . . . it's a question, you
said, of the *easement.* I don't underst . . . it's not
the *whole agreement.* It's just the *easement,* why
would she? Put, put, put, *Jerry* on. (*Pause*) Jer,
Jerry: What the *Hell* . . . that's my *house.* That's
. . . Well, I'm, no, no, no, I'm *not* coming ddd
. . . List, *Listen, screw* her. You *tell* her. You,
listen: I want you to take *Grace,* you take Grace,
and get out of that house. You *leave* her there.
Her and her lawyer, and you *tell* them, we'll see
them in court next . . . no. No. Leave her there,
leave her to *stew* in it: You tell her, we're *getting*
that house, and we are going to . . . No. I'm *not*
coming down. I'll be damned if I'll sit in the
same rrr . . . the next, you tell her the next time
I *see* her is in court . . . I . . . (*Pause*) What? (*Pause*)
What? I don't understand. (*Pause*) Well, what
about the house? (*Pause*) There isn't any problem
with the hhh . . . (*Pause*) No, no, no, that's all
right. All ri . . . All right . . . (*Pause*) Of course.
Tha . . . Thank you. No, I will. Right away. (*He
hangs up.*) (*Pause*)

CAROL: What is it? (*Pause*)

JOHN: It's a surprise party.

CAROL: It is.

JOHN: Yes.

CAROL: A party for you.

JOHN: Yes.

CAROL: Is it your birthday?

JOHN: No.

CAROL: What is it?

JOHN: The tenure announcement.

CAROL: The tenure announcement.

JOHN: They're throwing a party for us in our new house.

CAROL: Your new house.

JOHN: The house that we're buying.

CAROL: You have to go.

JOHN: It seems that I do.

CAROL: (*Pause*) They're proud of you.

JOHN: Well, there are those who would say it's a form
of aggression.

CAROL: What is?

JOHN: A surprise.

TWO

□□□

JOHN *and* CAROL *seated across the desk from each other.*

JOHN: You see, (*pause*) I love to teach. And flatter myself I am *skilled* at it. And I love the, the aspect of *performance*. I think I must confess that.

When I found I loved to teach I swore that I would not become that cold, rigid automaton of an instructor which I had encountered as a child.

Now, I was not unconscious that it was given me to err upon the other side. And, so, I asked and *ask* myself if I engaged in heterodoxy, I will not say "gratuitously" for I do not care to posit orthodoxy as a given good—but, "to the detriment of, of my students." (*Pause*)

As I said. When the possibility of tenure opened, and, of course, I'd long pursued it, I was, of course *happy,* and *covetous* of it.

I asked myself if I was wrong to covet it. And thought about it long, and, I hope, truthfully, and saw in myself several things in, I think, no particular order. (*Pause*)

That I *would* pursue it. That I *desired* it, that I was not pure of longing for security, and that that, perhaps, was not reprehensible in me. That I had duties *beyond* the school, and that my duty to my home, for instance, was, or should be, if it were not, of an equal weight. That tenure, and security, and yes, and *comfort,* were not, of themselves, to be scorned; and were even worthy of honorable pursuit. And that it was given me. Here, in this place, which I enjoy, and in which I find comfort, to assure myself of—as far as it rests in The Material—a continuation of that joy and comfort. In exchange for what? Teaching. Which I love.

What was the price of this security? To obtain *tenure.* Which tenure the committee is in the process of granting me. And on the basis of which I contracted to purchase a house. Now, as you don't have your own family, at this point, you may not know what that means. But to me it is important. A home. A Good Home. To raise my family. Now: The Tenure Committee will meet. This is the process, and a *good* process. Under which the school has functioned for quite a long time. They will meet, and hear your complaint—which you have the right to make; and they will dismiss it. They will *dismiss* your complaint; and, in the intervening period, I will lose my house. I will not be able to close on my house. I will lose my *deposit,* and the home I'd picked out for my wife and son will go by the boards. Now: I see I have angered you. I understand your anger at teachers. I was angry with mine. I felt hurt and humiliated by them. Which is one of the reasons that I went into education.

CAROL: What do you want of me?

JOHN: (*Pause*) I was hurt. When I received the report. Of the tenure committee. I was shocked. And I was hurt. No, I don't mean to subject you to my weak sensibilities. All right. Finally, I didn't understand. Then I thought: is it not always at those points at which we reckon ourselves unassailable that we are most vulnerable and . . . (*Pause*) Yes. All right. You find me pedantic. Yes. I am. By nature, by *birth,* by profession, I don't know . . . I'm always looking for a *paradigm* for . . .

CAROL: I don't know what a paradigm is.

JOHN: It's a model.

CAROL: Then why can't you use that word? (*Pause*)

JOHN: If it is important to you. Yes, all right. I was looking for a model. To continue: I feel that one point . . .

CAROL: I . . .

JOHN: One second . . . upon which I am unassailable is my unflinching concern for my students' dignity. I asked you here to . . . in the spirit of *investigation,* to ask you . . . to ask . . . (*Pause*) What have I done to you? (*Pause*) And, and, I suppose, how I can make amends. Can we not settle this now? It's pointless, really, and I want to know.

CAROL: What you can do to force me to retract?

JOHN: That is not what I meant at all.

CAROL: To bribe me, to convince me . . .

JOHN: . . . No.

CAROL: To retract . . .

JOHN: That is not what I meant at all. I think that you know it is not.

CAROL: That is not what I know. I *wish* I . . .

JOHN: I do not want to . . . you wish what?

CAROL: No, you said what amends can you make. To force me to retract.

JOHN: That is not what I said.

CAROL: I have my notes.

JOHN: Look. Look. The Stoics say . . .

CAROL: The Stoics?

JOHN: The Stoical Philosophers say if you remove the phrase "I have been injured," you have removed the injury. Now: Think: I know that you're upset. Just tell me. Literally. Literally: what wrong have I done you?

CAROL: Whatever you have done to me—to the extent that you've done it to *me,* do you know, rather than to me as a *student,* and, so, to the student body, is contained in my report. To the tenure committee.

JOHN: Well, all right. (*Pause*) Let's see. (*He reads.*) I find that I am sexist. That I am *elitist.* I'm not sure I know what that means, other than it's a derogatory word, meaning "bad." That I . . . That I insist on wasting time, in nonprescribed, in self-aggrandizing and theatrical *diversions* from the prescribed *text* . . . that these have taken both sexist and pornographic forms . . . here we find listed . . . (*Pause*) Here we find listed . . . instances ". . . closeted with a student" . . . "Told a rambling, sexually explicit story, in which the frequency and attitudes of fornication of the poor and rich are, it would seem, the central point . . . moved to *embrace* said student and . . . all part of a pattern . . ." (*Pause*)

(*He reads.*) That I used the phrase "The White Man's Burden" . . . that I told you how I'd asked you to my room because I quote like you. (*Pause*)

(*He reads.*) "He said he 'liked' me. That he 'liked being with me.' He'd let me write my examination paper over, if I could come back oftener to see him in his office." (*Pause*) (*To* CAROL:) It's *ludicrous*. Don't you know that? It's not *necessary*. It's going to *humiliate* you, and it's going to cost me my *house,* and . . .

CAROL: It's "*ludicrous* . . ."?

(JOHN *picks up the report and reads again.*)

JOHN: "He told me he had problems with his wife; and that he wanted to take off the artificial stricture of Teacher and Student. He put his arm around me . . ."

CAROL: Do you deny it? Can you deny it . . . ? Do you see? (*Pause*) Don't you see? You don't see, do you?

JOHN: I don't see . . .

CAROL: You think, you think you can deny that these things happened; or, if they *did,* if they *did,* that they meant what you *said* they meant. Don't you see? You drag me in here, you drag us, to listen to you "go on"; and "go on" about this, or that, or we don't "express" ourselves very well. We don't say what we mean. Don't we? Don't we? We *do* say what we mean. And you say that "I don't understand you . . .": Then *you* . . . (*Points.*)

JOHN: "Consult the Report"?

CAROL: . . . that's right.

JOHN: You see. You see. Can't you . . . . You see what I'm saying? Can't you tell me in your own words?

CAROL: Those are my own words. (*Pause*)

JOHN: (*He reads.*) "He told me that if I would stay alone with him in his office, he would change my grade to an A." (*To* CAROL:) What have I done to you? Oh. My God, are you so hurt?

CAROL: What I "feel" is irrelevant. (*Pause*)

JOHN: Do you know that I tried to help you?

CAROL: What I know I have reported.

JOHN: I would like to help you now. I would. Before this escalates.

CAROL (*simultaneously with* "escalates"): You see. I don't think that I need your help. I don't think I need anything you have.

JOHN: I feel . . .

CAROL: I don't *care* what you feel. Do you see? DO YOU SEE? You can't *do* that anymore. You. Do. Not. Have. The. Power. Did you misuse it? *Someone* did. Are you part of that group? *Yes*. *Yes*. You Are. You've *done* these things. And to say, and to say, "Oh. Let me help you with your problem . . ."

JOHN: Yes. I understand. I understand. You're *hurt*. You're *angry*. Yes. I think your *anger* is *betraying* you. Down a path which helps no one.

CAROL: I don't *care* what you think.

JOHN: You don't? (*Pause*) But you talk of *rights*. Don't you see? *I* have rights too. Do you see? I have a *house* . . . part of the *real* world; and The Tenure Committee, Good Men and True . . .

CAROL: . . . Professor . . .

JOHN: . . . Please: *Also* part of that world: you understand? This is my *life*. I'm not a *bogeyman*. I don't "stand" for something, I . . .

CAROL: . . . Professor . . .

JOHN: . . . I . . .

CAROL: Professor. I came here as a *favor*. At your personal request. Perhaps I should not have done so.

But I did. On my behalf, and on behalf of my group. And you speak of the tenure committee, one of whose members is a woman, as you know. And though you might call it Good Fun, or An Historical Phrase, or An Oversight, or, All of the Above, to refer to the committee as Good Men and True, it is a demeaning remark. It is a sexist remark, and to overlook it is to countenance continuation of that method of thought. It's a remark . . .

JOHN: OH COME ON. Come on. . . . Sufficient to deprive a family of . . .

CAROL: Sufficient? Sufficient? Sufficient? Yes. It is a *fact* . . . and that story, which I quote, is *vile* and *classist*, and *manipulative* and *pornographic*. It . . .

JOHN: . . . it's pornographic . . . ?

CAROL: What gives you the *right*. Yes. To speak to a *woman* in your private . . . Yes. Yes. I'm sorry. I'm sorry. You feel yourself empowered . . . you say so yourself. To *strut*. To *posture*. To "perform." To "Call me in here . . ." Eh? You say that higher education is a joke. And treat it as such, you *treat* it as such. And *confess* to a taste to play the *Patriarch* in your class. To grant *this*. To deny *that*. To embrace your students.

JOHN: How can you assert. How can you stand there and . . .

CAROL: How can you *deny* it. You did it to me. *Here.* You *did* . . . . You *confess.* You love the Power. To *deviate.* To *invent,* to transgress . . . to *transgress* whatever norms have been established for us. And you think it's charming to "question" in yourself this taste to mock and destroy. But you should question it. Professor. And you pick those things which you feel *advance* you: publication, *tenure,* and the steps to get them you call "harmless rituals." And you perform those steps. Although you say it is hypocrisy. But to the aspirations of your students. Of *hardworking students,* who come here, who *slave* to come here— you have no idea what it cost me to come to this school—you *mock* us. You call education "hazing," and from your so-protected, so-elitist seat you hold our confusion as a *joke,* and our hopes and efforts with it. Then you sit there and say "what have I done?" And ask me to understand that *you* have aspirations too. But I tell you. I tell you. That you are vile. And that you are exploitative. And if you possess one ounce of that inner honesty you describe in your book, you can look in yourself and see those things that I see. And you can find revulsion equal to my own. Good day. (*She prepares to leave the room.*)

JOHN: Wait a second, will you, just one moment. (*Pause*) Nice day today.

CAROL: What?

JOHN: You said "Good day." I think that it is a nice day today.

CAROL: *Is* it?

JOHN: Yes, I think it is.

CAROL: And why is that important?

JOHN: Because it is the essence of all human communication. I say something conventional, you respond, and the information we exchange is not about the "weather," but that we both agree to converse. In effect, we agree that we are both human. (*Pause*)

I'm not a . . . "exploiter," and you're not a . . . "deranged," what? *Revolutionary* . . . that we may, that we may have . . . positions, and that we may have . . . desires, which are in *conflict,* but that we're just human. (*Pause*) That means that sometimes we're *imperfect.* (*Pause*) Often we're in conflict . . . (*Pause*) *Much* of what we do, you're right, in the name of "principles" is *self-serving* . . . much of what we do is *conventional.* (*Pause*) You're right. (*Pause*) You said you came in the class because you wanted to learn about *education.* I don't know that I can teach you about education. But I know that I can tell you what I *think* about education, and then *you* decide. And you don't have to fight with me. *I'm* not the subject. (*Pause*) And where I'm *wrong* . . . per-

haps it's not your job to "fix" me. I don't want
to fix *you*. I would like to tell you what I *think,*
because that *is* my job, conventional as it is, and
flawed as I may be. And then, if you can show
me some better *form,* then we can proceed from
there. But, just like "nice day, isn't it . . . ?" I
don't think we can proceed until we accept that
each of us is human. (*Pause*) And we still can
have difficulties. We *will* have them . . . that's all
right too. (*Pause*) Now:

CAROL: . . . wait . . .

JOHN: Yes. I want to hear it.

CAROL: . . . the . . .

JOHN: Yes. Tell me frankly.

CAROL: . . . my position . . .

JOHN: I want to hear it. In your own words. What
you want. And what you feel.

CAROL: . . . I . . .

JOHN: . . . yes . . .

CAROL: My Group.

JOHN: Your "Group" . . . ? (*Pause*)

CAROL: The people I've been talking to . . .

JOHN: There's no shame in that. Everybody needs advisers. Everyone needs to expose themselves. To various points of view. It's not wrong. It's essential. Good. Good. Now: You and I . . . (*The phone rings.*)

You and I . . .

(*He hesitates for a moment, and then picks it up.*) (*Into phone*) Hello. (*Pause*) Um . . . no, I know they do. (*Pause*) I know she does. Tell her that I . . . can I call you back? . . . Then tell her that I think it's going to be fine. (*Pause*) Tell her just, just hold on, I'll . . . can I get back to you? . . . Well . . . no, no, no, we're *taking* the house . . . we're . . . no, no, nn . . . no, she will nnn, it's not a *question* of refunding the dep . . . no . . . it's not a *question* of the deposit . . . will you call Jerry? Babe, baby, will you just call Jerry? Tell him, nnn . . . tell him they, well, they're to keep the deposit, because the deal, be . . . because the deal is going to go *through* . . . because I know . . . be . . . will you please? Just *trust* me. Be . . . well, I'm dealing with the complaint. Yes. Right *Now*. Which is why I . . . yes, no, no, it's really, I can't *talk* about it now. Call Jerry, and I can't talk now. Ff . . . fine. Gg . . . good-bye. (*Hangs up.*) (*Pause*) I'm sorry we were interrupted.

CAROL: No . . .

JOHN: I . . . I was saying:

CAROL: You said that we should agree to talk about my complaint.

JOHN: That's correct.

CAROL: But we *are* talking about it.

JOHN: Well, that's correct too. You see? This is the *gist* of education.

CAROL: No, no. I mean, we're talking about it at the Tenure Committee Hearing. (*Pause*)

JOHN: Yes, but I'm saying: we can talk about it *now*, as easily as . . .

CAROL: No. I think that we should stick to the process . . .

JOHN: . . . wait a . . .

CAROL: . . . the "conventional" process. As you said. (*She gets up.*) And you're right, I'm sorry if I was, um, if I was "discourteous" to you. You're right.

JOHN: Wait, wait a . . .

CAROL: I really should go.

JOHN: Now, look, granted. I have an interest. In the status quo. All right? Everyone does. But what I'm saying is that the *committee* . . .

CAROL: Professor, you're right. Just don't impinge on me. We'll take our differences, and . . .

JOHN: You're going to make a . . . look, look, look, you're going to . . .

CAROL: I shouldn't have come here. They told me . . .

JOHN: One moment. No. No. There are *norms,* here, and there's no reason. Look: I'm trying to *save* you . . .

CAROL: No one *asked* you to . . . you're trying to save *me?* Do me the courtesy to . . .

JOHN: I *am* doing you the courtesy. I'm talking *straight* to you. We can settle this *now.* And I want you to sit *down* and . . .

CAROL: You must excuse me . . . (*She starts to leave the room.*)

JOHN: Sit down, it seems we each have a . . . . Wait one moment. Wait one moment . . . just do me the courtesy to . . .
(*He restrains her from leaving.*)

CAROL: LET ME GO.

JOHN: I have no desire to *hold* you, I just want to *talk* to you . . .

CAROL: LET ME GO. LET ME GO. WOULD SOMEBODY *HELP* ME? WOULD SOME-BODY *HELP* ME PLEASE . . . ?

THREE

□□□

(At rise, CAROL and JOHN are seated.)

JOHN: I have asked you here. (Pause) I have asked you
    here against, against my . . .

CAROL: I was most surprised you asked me.

JOHN: . . . against my better *judgment*, against . . .

CAROL: I was most surprised . . .

JOHN: . . . against the . . . yes. I'm sure.

CAROL: . . . If you would like me to leave, I'll leave.
    I'll go right now . . . (She rises.)

JOHN: Let us begin *correctly*, may we? I feel . . .

CAROL: That is what I wished to do. That's why I
    came here, but now . . .

JOHN: . . . I feel . . .

CAROL: But now perhaps you'd like me to leave . . .

JOHN: I don't want you to leave. I asked you to come . . .

CAROL: I didn't have to come here.

JOHN: No. (*Pause*) Thank you.

CAROL: All right. (*Pause*) (*She sits down.*)

JOHN: Although I feel that it *profits*, it would *profit* you something, to . . .

CAROL: . . . what I . . .

JOHN: If you would hear me out, if you would hear me out.

CAROL: I came here to, the court officers told me not to come.

JOHN: . . . the "court" officers . . . ?

CAROL: I was shocked that you asked.

JOHN: . . . wait . . .

CAROL: Yes. But I did *not* come here to hear what it "profits" me.

JOHN: The "court" officers . . .

CAROL: . . . no, no, perhaps I should leave . . . (*She gets up*.)

JOHN: Wait.

CAROL: No. I shouldn't have . . .

JOHN: . . . wait. Wait. Wait a moment.

CAROL: Yes? What is it you want? (*Pause*) What is it you want?

JOHN: I'd like you to stay.

CAROL: You want me to stay.

JOHN: Yes.

CAROL: You do.

JOHN: Yes. (*Pause*) Yes. I would like to have you hear me out. If you would. (*Pause*) Would you please? If you would do that I would be in your debt. (*Pause*) (*She sits.*) Thank You. (*Pause*)

CAROL: What is it you wish to tell me?

JOHN: All right. I cannot . . . (*Pause*) I cannot help but feel you are owed an apology. (*Pause*) (*Of papers in his hands*) I have read. (*Pause*) And reread these accusations.

CAROL: What "accusations"?

JOHN: The, the tenure comm . . . what other accusations . . . ?

CAROL: The tenure committee . . . ?

JOHN: Yes.

CAROL: Excuse me, but those are not accusations. They have been *proved*. They are facts.

JOHN: . . . I . . .

CAROL: No. Those are not "accusations."

JOHN: . . . those?

CAROL: . . . the committee (*The phone starts to ring*.) the committee has . . .

JOHN: . . . All right . . .

CAROL: . . . those are not accusations. The Tenure Committee.

JOHN: ALL RIGHT. ALL RIGHT. ALL RIGHT. (*He picks up the phone*.) Hello. Yes. No. I'm here. Tell Mister . . . No, I can't talk to him now . . . I'm sure he has, but I'm fff . . . I know . . . No, I have no time t . . . tell Mister . . . tell Mist . . . tell Jerry that I'm *fine* and that I'll call

him right aw . . . (*Pause*) My wife . . . Yes. I'm
sure she has. Yes, thank you. Yes, I'll call her
too. I cannot talk to you now. (*He hangs up.*)
(*Pause*) All right. It was good of you to come.
Thank you. I have studied. I have spent some
time studying the indictment.

CAROL: You will have to explain that word to me.

JOHN: An "indictment" . . .

CAROL: Yes.

JOHN: Is a "bill of particulars." A . . .

CAROL: All right. Yes.

JOHN: In which is alleged . . .

CAROL: No. I cannot allow that. I cannot allow that.
Nothing is alleged. Everything is proved . . .

JOHN: Please, wait a sec . . .

CAROL: I cannot *come* to allow . . .

JOHN: If I may . . . If I may, from whatever you feel
is "established," by . . .

CAROL: The issue here is not what I "feel." It is not
my "feelings," but the feelings of women. And
men. Your superiors, who've been "polled," do

you see? To whom *evidence* has been presented, who have *ruled*, do you see? Who have weighed the testimony and the evidence, and have *ruled*, do you see? That you are *negligent*. That you are *guilty*, that you are found *wanting*, and in *error;* and are *not*, for the reasons so-told, to be given tenure. That you are to be disciplined. For facts. For *facts*. Not "alleged," what is the word? But *proved*. Do you see? *By your own actions*.

That is what the tenure committee has said. That is what my lawyer said. For what you did in class. For what you did *in this office*.

JOHN: They're going to discharge me.

CAROL: As full well they should. You don't understand? You're angry? What has *led* you to this place? Not your sex. Not your race. Not your class. YOUR OWN ACTIONS. And you're *angry*. You *ask* me here. What *do* you want? You want to "charm" me. You want to "convince" me. You want me to recant. I will *not* recant. Why should I . . . ? What I say is right. You tell me, you are going to tell me that you have a wife and child. You are going to say that you have a career and that you've worked for twenty years for this. Do you know what you've *worked* for? *Power*. For *power*. Do you understand? And you sit there, and you tell me *stories*. About your *house*, about all the private *schools*, and about *privilege*, and how you are entitled. To *buy*, to *spend,* to *mock,* to *summon.* All your stories. All your silly weak *guilt,* it's all about *privilege;* and you won't know it. Don't you see? You worked twenty years for the right to *insult* me. And you feel entitled to be *paid* for it. Your Home. Your Wife . . . Your sweet "deposit" on your house . . .

JOHN: Don't you have feelings?

CAROL: That's my point. You see? Don't you have feelings? Your final argument. What is it that has no feelings. *Animals.* I don't take your side, you question if I'm Human.

JOHN: Don't you have feelings?

CAROL: I have a responsibility. I . . .

JOHN: . . . to . . . ?

CAROL: To? This institution. To the *students.* To my *group.*

JOHN: . . . your "group." . . .

CAROL: Because I speak, yes, not for myself. But for the group; for those who suffer what I suffer. On behalf of whom, even if I, were, inclined, to what, forgive? Forget? What? Overlook your . . .

JOHN: . . . my behavior?

CAROL: . . . it would be wrong.

JOHN: Even if you were inclined to "forgive" me.

CAROL: It would be wrong.

JOHN: And what would transpire.

CAROL: Transpire?

JOHN: Yes.

CAROL: "Happen?"

JOHN: Yes.

CAROL: Then *say* it. For Christ's sake. Who the *hell* do you think that you are? You want a post. You want unlimited power. To do and to say what you want. As it pleases you—Testing, Questioning, Flirting . . .

JOHN: I never . . .

CAROL: Excuse me, one moment, will you?
   (*She reads from her notes.*)
      The twelfth: "Have a good day, dear."
      The fifteenth: "Now, don't *you* look fetching . . ."
      April seventeenth: "If you girls would come over here . . ." I saw you. I saw you, Professor. For two semesters sit there, stand there and ex-

ploit our, as you thought, "paternal prerogative," and what is that but rape; I swear to God. You asked me in here to explain something to me, as a child, that I did not understand. But I came to explain something to you. You Are Not God. You ask me why I came? I came here to instruct you.

(*She produces his book.*)

And your book? You think you're going to show me some "light"? You *"maverick."* Outside of tradition. No, no, (*She reads from the book's liner notes.*) *"of* that fine tradition of *inquiry.* Of Polite *skepticism"* . . . and you say you believe in free intellectual discourse. YOU BELIEVE IN NOTHING. YOU BELIEVE IN NOTHING AT ALL.

JOHN: I believe in freedom of thought.

CAROL: Isn't that fine. *Do* you?

JOHN: Yes. I do.

CAROL: Then why do you question, for one moment, the committee's decision refusing your tenure? Why do you question your suspension? You believe in what *you call* freedom of thought. Then, fine. *You* believe in freedom-of-thought *and* a home, and, *and* prerogatives for your kid, *and* tenure. And I'm going to tell you. You believe *not* in "freedom of thought," but in an elitist, in, in a protected hierarchy which rewards you. And for whom you are the clown. And you mock and exploit the system which pays your rent. You're wrong. I'm not wrong. You're wrong. You think that I'm full of hatred. I know what you think I am.

JOHN: Do you?

CAROL: You think I'm a, of course I do. You think I am a frightened, repressed, confused, I don't know, abandoned young thing of some doubtful sexuality, who wants, power and revenge. (*Pause*) *Don't* you? (*Pause*)

JOHN: Yes. I do. (*Pause*)

CAROL: Isn't that better? And I feel that that is the first moment which you've treated me with respect. For you told me the truth. (*Pause*) I did not come here, as you are assured, to gloat. Why would I want to gloat? I've profited nothing from your, your, as you say, your "misfortune." I came here, as you did me the honor to *ask* me here, I came here to *tell* you something.

(*Pause*) That I think . . . that I think you've been wrong. That I think you've been terribly wrong. Do you hate me now? (*Pause*)

JOHN: Yes.

CAROL: Why do you hate me? Because you think me wrong? No. Because I have, you think, *power* over you. Listen to me. Listen to me, Professor. (*Pause*) It is the power that you hate. So deeply that, that any atmosphere of free discussion is impossible. It's not "unlikely." It's *impossible*. Isn't it?

JOHN: Yes.

CAROL: *Isn't* it . . . ?

JOHN: Yes. I suppose.

CAROL: Now. The thing which you find so cruel is the selfsame process of selection I, and my group, go through *every day of our lives*. In admittance to school. In our tests, in our class rankings. . . . Is it unfair? I can't tell you. But, if it is fair. Or even if it is "unfortunate but necessary" for us, then, by God, so must it be for you. (*Pause*) You write of your "responsibility to the young." Treat us with respect, and that will *show* you your responsibility. You write that education is just hazing. (*Pause*) But we worked to get to this school. (*Pause*) And some of us. (*Pause*) Overcame prejudices. Economic, sexual, you cannot begin to imagine. And endured humiliations I *pray* that you and those you love never will encounter. (*Pause*) To gain admittance here. To pursue that same dream of security *you* pursue. We, who, who are, at any moment, in danger of being deprived of it. By . . .

JOHN: . . . by . . . ?

CAROL: By the administration. By the teachers. By *you*. By, say, one low grade, that keeps us out of graduate school; by one, say, one capricious or inventive answer on our parts, which, perhaps, you don't find amusing. Now you *know,* do you see? What it is to be subject to that power. (*Pause*)

JOHN: I don't understand. (*Pause*)

CAROL: My charges are not trivial. You see that in the haste, I think, with which they were accepted. A *joke* you have told, with a sexist tinge. The language you use, a verbal or physical caress, yes, yes, I know, you say that it is meaningless. I understand. I differ from you. To lay a hand on someone's shoulder.

JOHN: It was devoid of sexual content.

CAROL: I say it was not. I SAY IT WAS NOT. Don't you begin to *see* . . . ? Don't you begin to understand? IT'S NOT FOR YOU TO SAY.

JOHN: I take your point, and I see there is much good in what you refer to.

CAROL: . . . do you think so . . . ?

JOHN: . . . but, and this is not to say that I cannot change, in those things in which I am deficient . . . But, the . . .

CAROL: Do you hold yourself harmless from the charge of sexual exploitativeness . . . ? (*Pause*)

JOHN: Well, I . . . I . . . I . . . You know I, as I said. I . . . think I am not too old to *learn,* and I *can* learn, I . . .

CAROL: Do you hold yourself innocent of the charge of . . .

JOHN: . . . wait, wait, wait . . . All right, let's go back to . . .

CAROL: YOU FOOL. Who do you think I am? To come here and be taken in by a *smile.* You little yapping fool. You think I want "revenge." I don't want revenge. I WANT UNDER-STANDING.

JOHN: . . . *do* you?

CAROL: I do. (*Pause*)

JOHN: What's the use. It's over.

CAROL: Is it? What is?

JOHN: My job.

CAROL: Oh. Your job. That's what you want to talk about. (*Pause*) (*She starts to leave the room. She steps and turns back to him.*) All right. (*Pause*) What if it were possible that my Group withdraws its complaint. (*Pause*)

JOHN: What?

CAROL: That's right. (*Pause*)

JOHN: Why.

CAROL: Well, let's say as an act of friendship.

JOHN: An act of friendship.

CAROL: Yes. (*Pause*)

JOHN: In exchange for what.

CAROL: Yes. But I don't think, "exchange." Not "in exchange." For what do we derive from it? (*Pause*)

JOHN: "Derive."

CAROL: Yes.

JOHN: (*Pause*) Nothing. (*Pause*)

CAROL: That's right. We derive nothing. (*Pause*) Do you see that?

JOHN: Yes.

CAROL: That is a little word, Professor. "Yes." "I see that." But you will.

JOHN: And you might speak to the committee . . . ?

CAROL: To the committee?

JOHN: Yes.

CAROL: Well. Of course. That's on your mind. We might.

JOHN: "If" what?

CAROL: "Given" what. Perhaps. I think that that is more friendly.

JOHN: GIVEN WHAT?

CAROL: And, believe me, I understand your rage. It is not that I don't feel it. But I do not see that it is deserved, so I do not resent it . . . . All right. I have a list.

JOHN: . . . a list.

CAROL: Here is a list of books, which we . . .

JOHN: . . . a list of books . . . ?

CAROL: That's right. Which we find questionable.

JOHN: What?

CAROL: Is this so bizarre . . . ?

JOHN: I can't believe . . .

CAROL: It's not necessary you believe it.

JOHN: Academic freedom . . .

CAROL: Someone chooses the books. If you can choose them, others can. What are you, "God"?

JOHN: . . . no, no, the "dangerous." . . .

CAROL: You have an agenda, we have an agenda. I am not interested in your feelings or your motivation, but your actions. If you would like me to speak to the Tenure Committee, here is my list. You are a Free Person, you decide. (*Pause*)

JOHN: Give me the list. (*She does so. He reads.*)

CAROL: I think you'll find . . .

JOHN: I'm capable of reading it. Thank you.

CAROL: We have a number of *texts* we need re . . .

JOHN: I see that.

CAROL: We're amenable to . . .

JOHN: Aha. Well, let me look over the . . . (*He reads.*)

74

CAROL: I think that . . .

JOHN: LOOK. I'm reading your demands. All right?!
(*He reads*) (*Pause*) You want to ban my book?

CAROL: We do not . . .

JOHN (*Of list*): It says here . . .

CAROL: . . . We want it removed from inclusion as a
representative example of the university.

JOHN: Get out of here.

CAROL: If you put aside the issues of personalities.

JOHN: Get the fuck out of my office.

CAROL: No, I think I would reconsider.

JOHN: . . . you think you can.

CAROL: We can and we *will*. Do you want our support? That is the only quest . . .

JOHN: . . . to ban my *book* . . . ?

CAROL: . . . that is correct . . .

JOHN: . . . this . . . this is a *university* . . . we . . .

CAROL: . . . and we have a statement . . . which we
need you to . . . (*She hands him a sheet of paper.*)

JOHN: No, no. It's out of the question. I'm sorry. I don't know what I was thinking of. I want to tell you something. I'm a teacher. I am a teacher. Eh? It's my *name* on the door, and *I* teach the class, and that's what I do. I've got a book with my name on it. And my son will *see* that *book* someday. And I have a respon . . . No, I'm sorry I have a *responsibility* . . . to *myself*, to my *son*, to my *profession*. . . . I haven't been *home* for two days, do you know that? Thinking this out.

CAROL: . . . you haven't?

JOHN: I've been, no. If it's of interest to you. I've been in a *hotel*. *Thinking*. (*The phone starts ringing*.) *Thinking* . . .

CAROL: . . . you haven't been home?

JOHN: . . . *thinking,* do you see.

CAROL: Oh.

JOHN: And, and, I owe you a debt, I see that now. (*Pause*) You're *dangerous,* you're *wrong* and it's my *job* . . . to say no to you. That's my job. You are absolutely right. You want to ban my book? Go to *hell,* and they can do whatever they want to me.

CAROL: . . . you haven't been home in two days . . .

JOHN: I think I told you that.

CAROL: . . . you'd better get that phone. (*Pause*) I think that you should pick up the phone. (*Pause*)

(JOHN *picks up the phone.*)

JOHN (*on phone*): Yes. (*Pause*) Yes. Wh . . . I. I. I had to be away. All ri . . . did they wor . . . did they worry ab . . . No. I'm all right, now, Jerry. I'm f . . . I got a little turned *around,* but I'm *sitting* here and . . . I've got it figured out. I'm fine. I'm fine don't worry about me. I got a little bit mixed up. But I am not sure that it's not a blessing. It cost me my job? Fine. Then the job was not worth having. Tell Grace that I'm coming home and everything is fff . . . (*Pause*) What? (*Pause*) *What?* (*Pause*) What do you *mean?* WHAT? Jerry . . . Jerry. They . . . Who, who, what can they do . . . ? (*Pause*) NO. (*Pause*) NO. They can't do th . . . What do you mean? (*Pause*) But how . . . (*Pause*) She's, she's, she's *here* with me. To . . . Jerry. I don't underst . . . (*Pause*) (*He hangs up.*) (*To* CAROL:) What does this mean?

CAROL: I thought you knew.

JOHN: What. (*Pause*) What does it mean. (*Pause*)

CAROL: You tried to rape me. (*Pause*) According to the law. (*Pause*)

JOHN: . . . what . . . ?

CAROL: You tried to rape me. I was leaving this office, you "pressed" yourself into me. You "pressed" your body into me.

JOHN: . . . I . . .

CAROL: My Group has told your lawyer that we may pursue criminal charges.

JOHN: . . . no . . .

CAROL: . . . under the statute. I am told. It was battery.

JOHN: . . . no . . .

CAROL: Yes. And attempted rape. That's right. (*Pause*)

JOHN: I think that you should go.

CAROL: Of course. I thought you knew.

JOHN: I have to talk to my lawyer.

CAROL: Yes. Perhaps you should.
        (*The phone rings again.*) (*Pause*)

JOHN: (*Picks up phone. Into phone:*) Hello? I . . . Hello
        . . . ? I . . . Yes, he just called. No . . . I. I can't
        talk to you now, Baby. (*To* CAROL:) Get out.

CAROL: . . . your wife . . . ?

JOHN: . . . who it is is no concern of yours. Get out. (*To phone:*) No, no, it's going to be all right. I. I can't talk now, Baby. (*To* CAROL:) Get out of here.

CAROL: I'm going.

JOHN: Good.

CAROL (*exiting*): . . . and don't call your wife "baby."

JOHN: What?

CAROL: Don't call your wife baby. You heard what I said.

(CAROL *starts to leave the room.* JOHN *grabs her and begins to beat her.*)

JOHN: You vicious little bitch. You think you can come in here with your political correctness and destroy my life?

(*He knocks her to the floor.*)

After how I treated you . . . ? You should be . . . *Rape you* . . . ? Are you kidding me . . . ?

(*He picks up a chair, raises it above his head, and advances on her.*)

I wouldn't touch you with a ten-foot pole. You little *cunt* . . .

(*She cowers on the floor below him. Pause. He looks down at her. He lowers the chair. He moves to his desk, and arranges the papers on it. Pause. He looks over at her.*)

. . . well . . .

(*Pause. She looks at him.*)

CAROL: Yes. That's right.

(*She looks away from him, and lowers her head. To herself:*) . . . yes. That's right.

END